Navigating the Job Market:
How Students Can Develop Marketable Skills

Taylor Linton

To OK and HR, my best little buddies

Table Of Contents

Chapter 1: Understanding the Job Market
- The Current Job Market Landscape
- Identifying In-Demand Skills
- The Importance of Marketable Skills

Chapter 2: Today's Marketable Skills
- Becoming a Bookkeeper
- Learning to Code
- Starting a Career in Marketing
- Learning to Analyze Data
- Content Creation and Management
- Marketable Soft Skills

Chapter 3: Assessing Your Skills and Interests
- Self Assessment Tools
- Identifying Transferable Skills
- Exploring Career Paths

Chapter 4: Developing Marketable Skills
- Acquiring Industry-Relevant Certifications
- Building Technical Skills
- Enhancing Soft Skills

Chapter 5: Gaining Practical Experience
- Internships and Co-op Opportunities
- Volunteer Work and Extracurriculars
- Networking and Mentorship

Chapter 6: Showcasing Your Skills to Employers
- Build a strong Resume
- Crafting a Compelling Cover Letter
- Crafting an Impressive Portfolio

Chapter 7: Navigating the Job Search Process
- Job Search Strategies

- Interview Preparation
- Negotiating Job Offers

Chapter 8: Continuous Learning and Skill Development
- Lifelong Learning Opportunities
- Professional Development Resources
- Staying Relevant in a Changing Job Market

Chapter 9: Overcoming Challenges in the Job Market
- Dealing with Rejection
- Addressing Skill Gaps
- Managing Career Transitions

Chapter 10: Success Stories and Advice From Industry Professionals
- Insight From Successful Professionals
- Tips for Career Advancement
- Lessons from Real-World Experiences

Chapter 11: Conclusion
- Recap of Key Points
- Final Thoughts and Action Steps
- Resources for Further Exploration

Afterword

Chapter 1: Understanding the Job Market

The Current Job Market Landscape

  The current job market landscape is constantly evolving, with new trends and technologies shaping the way companies hire and recruit talent. As students looking to enter the workforce, it is important to stay informed about the latest developments in the job market in order to develop the skills that will make you stand out to potential employers. In this subchapter, we will explore some of the key trends in the job market and discuss how you can position yourself for success.

One of the biggest trends in the job market today is the increasing demand for candidates with technical skills. As technology continues to play a larger role in virtually every industry, employers are looking for candidates who can demonstrate proficiency in areas such as data analysis, coding, and digital marketing. By developing these technical skills, you can make yourself a more attractive candidate to potential employers and increase your chances of landing a job in a competitive market.

  In addition to technical skills, employers are also placing a premium on soft skills such as communication, problem-solving, and teamwork. These skills are essential for success in any job, as they enable you to work effectively with others and adapt to changing circumstances. By honing your soft skills, you can demonstrate to employers that you are a well-rounded candidate who can thrive in a variety of work environments.

Another important trend in the job market is the rise of remote work opportunities. With advancements in technology making it easier than ever for employees to work from anywhere, many companies are offering remote work options to attract top talent. As a student, this trend presents you with the opportunity to explore job opportunities outside of your immediate geographic area and find a job that aligns with your lifestyle preferences.

Finally, it is important to remember that the job market is highly competitive, and simply having the right skills may not be enough to secure a job. Networking and building relationships with industry professionals can often be the key to finding job opportunities and advancing your career. By attending networking events, connecting with alumni, and building a strong online presence, you can increase your chances of landing your dream job in a competitive job market.

Identifying In-Demand Skills

In today's competitive job market, it is essential for students to identify and develop in-demand skills that will set them apart from other candidates. By focusing on acquiring these skills, students can increase their chances of landing their dream job and advancing in their careers. In this subchapter, we will explore some of the most sought-after skills in the job market and provide tips on how students can develop and showcase these skills to potential employers.

One of the most in-demand skills in today's job market is problem-solving. Employers are looking for candidates who can think critically, analyze complex situations, and come up with creative solutions to challenges. To develop this skill, students can participate in problem-solving activities, such as case studies, group projects, and internships. By honing their problem-solving abilities, students can demonstrate to employers that they have the capacity to tackle difficult issues and drive innovation within the company.

Another highly sought-after skill is communication. Effective communication is key in any workplace, as it enables individuals to convey ideas clearly, collaborate with others, and build strong relationships with colleagues and clients. Students can enhance their communication skills by participating in public speaking events, writing workshops, and networking opportunities. By becoming proficient communicators, students can showcase their ability to articulate their thoughts, work well with others, and represent their organization in a professional manner.

      In addition to problem-solving and communication skills, employers are also looking for candidates who possess strong technical skills. In today's digital age, proficiency in technology is essential for success in many industries. Students can develop their technical skills by taking courses in programming languages, software applications, and data analysis tools. By acquiring these skills, students can demonstrate to employers that they are adept at using technology to streamline processes, analyze data, and drive business growth.

      Furthermore, adaptability and flexibility are crucial skills that are highly valued in the job market. With the rapid pace of change in today's business world, employers are seeking candidates who can quickly adapt to new situations, learn new skills, and pivot when necessary. Students can demonstrate their adaptability by taking on new challenges, volunteering for diverse projects, and seeking out opportunities for growth and development. By showcasing their ability to adapt to change, students can position themselves as valuable assets to potential employers.

In conclusion, by identifying and developing in-demand skills such as problem-solving, communication, technical proficiency, and adaptability, students can increase their marketability and stand out in the job market. By honing these skills through coursework, internships, extracurricular activities, and networking opportunities, students can position themselves for success in their chosen field. By focusing on developing these skills, students can enhance their chances of securing their desired job and thriving in their careers.

The Importance of Marketable Skills

In today's competitive job market, it is essential for students to develop marketable skills that will set them apart from the competition. Marketable skills are abilities, knowledge, and experiences that are valuable to employers and can help students stand out when applying for jobs. These skills not only increase a student's chances of securing employment but also contribute to their overall professional development.

One of the key reasons why marketable skills are important is that they make students more attractive to potential employers. When employers see that a student possesses a certain set of skills that are relevant to the job they are applying for, they are more likely to consider them for the position. Marketable skills can include technical skills, such as proficiency in a particular software program, as well as soft skills, like communication and problem-solving abilities. By developing a diverse range of marketable skills, students can increase their chances of landing their dream job.

Furthermore, having marketable skills can also lead to higher earning potential. Employers are often willing to pay more for candidates who bring valuable skills to the table. By investing time and effort into developing marketable skills, students can position themselves for higher-paying job opportunities in their chosen field. Additionally, possessing marketable skills can also lead to greater job security, as students who have in-demand skills are less likely to be laid off or replaced by automation.

Another important aspect of marketable skills is that they can help students adapt to a rapidly changing job market. As technology continues to advance and industries evolve, the skills that are in demand are constantly shifting. By staying up-to-date with the latest trends in their field and continually developing new marketable skills, students can ensure that they remain competitive in the job market. This adaptability is crucial for long-term career success and can help students navigate the ever-changing landscape of the job market.

    In conclusion, developing marketable skills is essential for students who want to succeed in today's job market. These skills not only make students more attractive to employers but also increase their earning potential and job security. By investing in their professional development and continuously acquiring new marketable skills, students can position themselves for success in their chosen field. Ultimately, marketable skills are the key to standing out in a crowded job market and securing a fulfilling and rewarding career.

Chapter 2: Today's Marketable Skills

Becoming a Bookkeeper

Becoming a bookkeeper is a valuable skill that can open up many opportunities in the job market. Bookkeepers are responsible for maintaining financial records for businesses, which includes recording transactions, balancing accounts, and preparing financial statements. This role requires attention to detail, strong organizational skills, and a solid understanding of accounting principles. By becoming a bookkeeper, students can develop a highly marketable skillset that is in demand across various industries.

To become a bookkeeper, students should consider pursuing a degree or certification in accounting or bookkeeping. Many colleges and universities offer programs specifically designed to prepare students for a career in bookkeeping. These programs typically cover topics such as financial accounting, managerial accounting, and tax preparation. Additionally, students can also pursue certifications such as the Certified Bookkeeper (CB) designation, which can further enhance their credibility and marketability as a bookkeeper.

In addition to formal education, gaining hands-on experience is essential for becoming a successful bookkeeper. Students can seek out internships or part-time positions in accounting firms or businesses that require bookkeeping services. This practical experience will not only enhance their skills but also provide valuable insights into the day-to-day responsibilities of a bookkeeper. Furthermore, students can also consider volunteering for non-profit organizations or small businesses to gain additional experience and build their professional network.

Networking is another important aspect of becoming a bookkeeper. Students should attend industry events, join professional organizations such as the American Institute of Professional Bookkeepers (AIPB), and connect with professionals in the field through social media platforms like LinkedIn. Building a strong network can help students learn about job opportunities, gain mentorship from experienced bookkeepers, and stay updated on industry trends and best practices. By actively networking, students can increase their chances of landing a job as a bookkeeper and advancing their career in the field.

Overall, becoming a bookkeeper is a valuable skill that can lead to a rewarding career with ample opportunities for growth and advancement. By pursuing a formal education, gaining practical experience, and actively networking, students can develop the necessary skills and knowledge to succeed as a bookkeeper in today's competitive job market. With dedication and hard work, students can position themselves as in-demand professionals with a highly marketable skillset that is essential for businesses of all sizes and industries.

Learning to Code

In today's job market, having the ability to code is becoming an increasingly valuable skill. Whether you are interested in pursuing a career in technology, marketing, finance, or any other field, learning to code can open up a world of opportunities for you. In this subchapter, we will explore the importance of learning to code and provide some tips and resources for students who are interested in developing this valuable skill.

One of the key reasons why learning to code is so important is that it can help you stand out to potential employers. In a competitive job market, having coding skills on your resume can set you apart from other candidates and demonstrate your ability to think logically, solve complex problems, and work independently. Employers are increasingly looking for candidates who have technical skills, so learning to code can give you a significant advantage in the job market.

Additionally, learning to code can also help you develop valuable problem-solving skills that can be applied to a wide range of professional situations. Coding requires you to break down complex problems into smaller, more manageable parts, identify patterns and trends, and come up with creative solutions. These problem-solving skills are highly transferable and can be applied to almost any job or industry, making coding a valuable skill to have in your toolkit.

If you are interested in learning to code, there are a wide range of resources available to help you get started. Online learning platforms like Codecademy, Khan Academy, and Coursera offer free or low-cost courses in a variety of programming languages, from Python and Java to HTML and CSS. Additionally, many universities and community colleges offer coding bootcamps and workshops for students who want to dive deeper into the world of programming.

In conclusion, learning to code is a valuable skill that can help you stand out in today's competitive job market and develop important problem-solving skills that will serve you well throughout your career. By taking the time to learn to code and practicing regularly, you can increase your marketability to potential employers and open up new opportunities for yourself in a wide range of industries. So don't wait – start learning to code today and take your career to the next level!

Starting a Career in Marketing

Marketing is a dynamic and fast-paced field that offers a wide range of opportunities for individuals with strong communication, creativity, and analytical skills. If you are interested in pursuing a career in marketing, there are several steps you can take to start building the skills and experience you need to succeed in this competitive industry.

One of the first things you can do to kickstart your marketing career is to gain hands-on experience through internships or part-time jobs. Many companies offer internships in marketing departments that can provide valuable real-world experience and help you build a network of industry contacts. Look for opportunities to work on marketing campaigns, conduct market research, and analyze consumer behavior to gain a better understanding of the field.

In addition to gaining practical experience, it is important to also develop your skills in areas such as social media marketing, digital advertising, and content creation. Taking courses or workshops in these areas can help you stay current with industry trends and technologies, and make you a more competitive candidate for marketing positions. Building a portfolio of your work, such as social media campaigns or marketing materials you have created, can also demonstrate your skills to potential employers.

Networking is another important factor in starting a career in marketing. Attending industry events, joining professional organizations, and connecting with marketing professionals on platforms like LinkedIn can help you expand your network and learn from others in the field. Networking can also help you discover job opportunities that may not be advertised publicly, giving you an edge in the job market.

Finally, it is important to stay informed about the latest trends and developments in the marketing industry. Reading marketing blogs, attending webinars, and following industry leaders on social media can help you stay current with best practices and emerging technologies. By continuously learning and adapting to changes in the field, you can position yourself as a knowledgeable and skilled marketing professional ready to take on new challenges and opportunities.

Learning to Analyze Data

In today's job market, having the ability to analyze data is a highly sought-after skill that can set you apart from other candidates. Whether you are applying for a job in marketing, finance, or any other field, being able to interpret and make sense of data is essential. In this subchapter, we will explore the importance of learning to analyze data and provide you with tips on how to develop this valuable skill.

Data analysis involves collecting, organizing, and interpreting data to make informed decisions. By analyzing data, you can identify trends, patterns, and correlations that can help you understand a problem or situation better. This skill is crucial in a variety of industries, as companies rely on data to make strategic decisions and drive business growth. By mastering data analysis, you can become a valuable asset to any organization.

To excel in data analysis, it is important to have a strong foundation in statistics and mathematics. Understanding concepts such as probability, regression analysis, and hypothesis testing will help you interpret data accurately and draw meaningful conclusions. Additionally, familiarity with data analysis tools such as

Excel, R, and Python can enhance your ability to manipulate and visualize data effectively.

One of the best ways to improve your data analysis skills is to practice regularly. Look for opportunities to work on real-world data sets, either through internships, class projects, or online courses. By applying your knowledge in a practical setting, you can hone your analytical skills and gain hands-on experience that will be valuable to future employers. Don't be afraid to challenge yourself and tackle complex data problems – the more you practice, the better you will become at analyzing data.

In conclusion, learning to analyze data is a valuable skill that can open up a world of opportunities in the job market. By developing your proficiency in data analysis, you can increase your marketability and stand out as a candidate with valuable skills. Take the time to build a strong foundation in statistics and mathematics, practice regularly, and familiarize yourself with data analysis tools. With dedication and perseverance, you can become a skilled data analyst who is in high demand in today's competitive job market.

Content Creation and Management

In today's digital age, content creation and management have become essential skills for any job seeker looking to stand out in the competitive job market. As students, it is crucial to develop these skills early on to enhance your marketability and increase your chances of landing your dream job. This subchapter will explore the importance of content creation and management in the job market, as well as provide tips and strategies for developing and showcasing these skills effectively.

Content creation involves the process of generating original and engaging material for various platforms, such as websites, social media, and marketing campaigns. By creating compelling content, you can demonstrate your creativity, critical thinking, and communication skills to potential employers. Whether you are writing blog posts, designing infographics, or producing videos, it is important to tailor your content to your target audience and brand voice. Additionally, learning how to use content management systems like WordPress or Squarespace can help you organize and publish your content efficiently.

Effective content management involves organizing, editing, and optimizing your content to ensure it reaches the right audience and achieves your desired goals. By developing strong organizational skills and attention to detail, you can streamline your content creation process and maintain a consistent brand image across all platforms. It is also important to stay up-to-date on industry trends and best practices in content management to ensure your content remains relevant and engaging. By mastering content management tools like Hootsuite or Buffer, you can schedule and analyze your content performance to make data-driven decisions for future content creation.

    One of the key benefits of mastering content creation and management is the ability to showcase your skills and experience to potential employers. By creating a professional portfolio or personal blog showcasing your best work, you can demonstrate your expertise and creativity to recruiters and hiring managers. Additionally, participating in content creation projects or internships can provide valuable hands-on experience and networking opportunities in your desired field. By building a strong online presence and showcasing your content creation and management skills, you can differentiate yourself from other job seekers and increase your chances of landing interviews and job offers.

In conclusion, content creation and management are essential skills for students looking to develop marketable skills and succeed in the job market. By honing your creativity, organization, and communication skills through content creation, you can demonstrate your value to potential employers and stand out from the competition. Whether you are interested in pursuing a career in marketing, journalism, or digital media, mastering content creation and management can open up a world of opportunities and help you achieve your professional goals. Start building your content creation and management skills today to navigate the job market with confidence and success.

Marketable Soft Skills

In today's competitive job market, having technical skills alone is not enough to stand out to potential employers. Soft skills, which are often referred to as interpersonal or transferable skills, play a crucial role in securing a job and excelling in the workplace. These skills are highly sought after by employers as they demonstrate an individual's ability to work well with others, communicate effectively, and adapt to different situations. In this subchapter, we will explore some of the most marketable soft skills that students can develop to enhance their employability.

One of the most important soft skills that students can cultivate is communication. Being able to effectively convey information, ideas, and feedback is essential in any job setting. Whether it's through written communication, verbal communication, or nonverbal cues, strong communication skills can help students build relationships with colleagues, clients, and supervisors. By honing their communication skills, students can become better team players, problem solvers, and leaders in the workplace.

Another marketable soft skill that students should focus on developing is adaptability. In today's fast-paced and ever-changing work environments, the ability to adapt to new challenges and situations is crucial. Being able to think on your feet, pivot when necessary, and embrace change can set students apart from their peers. Employers value individuals who are flexible, open-minded, and resilient in the face of uncertainty.

Collaboration is another key soft skill that students should prioritize. Working effectively with others towards a common goal is essential in today's team-oriented workplaces. Students who can collaborate with diverse groups of people, communicate their ideas clearly, and contribute positively to group projects are highly valued by employers. By fostering their collaboration skills, students can enhance their ability to work well in a team and achieve success collectively.

Problem-solving is a soft skill that is highly sought after by employers across industries. Being able to identify issues, analyze situations, and come up with creative solutions is an invaluable asset in the workplace. Students who can demonstrate strong problem-solving skills are seen as proactive, resourceful, and innovative. By developing their problem-solving abilities, students can showcase their critical thinking skills and make meaningful contributions to their organizations.

Lastly, emotional intelligence is a soft skill that can set students apart in the job market. Emotional intelligence encompasses self-awareness, self-regulation, empathy, and social skills. Individuals who possess high emotional intelligence are able to understand and manage their own emotions, as well as navigate interpersonal relationships effectively. By cultivating their emotional intelligence, students can build strong connections with others, resolve conflicts peacefully, and thrive in diverse work environments. Overall, developing marketable soft skills is essential for students looking to succeed in the job market and advance in their careers.

By focusing on communication, adaptability, collaboration, problem-solving, and emotional intelligence, students can enhance their employability and stand out to potential employers.

Chapter 3: Assessing Your Skills and Interests

Self-Assessment Tools

Self-assessment tools are essential resources for students looking to develop their marketable skills and navigate the job market successfully. These tools provide individuals with the opportunity to reflect on their strengths, weaknesses, interests, and values in order to identify areas for growth and improvement. By utilizing self-assessment tools, students can gain a better understanding of themselves and their career goals, ultimately helping them make more informed decisions about their future.

One popular self-assessment tool is the Myers-Briggs Type Indicator (MBTI), which categorizes individuals into one of 16 personality types based on their preferences in four key areas: extraversion/introversion, sensing/intuition, thinking/feeling, and judging/perceiving. By taking the MBTI assessment, students can gain valuable insights into their personality traits and how they interact with others in various professional settings. This information can be incredibly useful when it comes to choosing a career path that aligns with their strengths and interests.

Another valuable self-assessment tool is the StrengthsFinder assessment, which helps individuals identify their top five strengths out of a list of 34 key attributes. By understanding their unique strengths, students can leverage these qualities in the workplace to excel in their chosen field. This self-awareness can also help students communicate their strengths effectively during job interviews and networking opportunities, increasing their chances of securing a desirable position.

In addition to personality and strengths assessments, students can also benefit from utilizing interest inventories to explore potential career paths that align with their passions and values. These assessments help individuals identify their hobbies, interests, and values, providing them with valuable information about potential industries and job roles that may be a good fit for them. By taking the time to reflect on their interests, students can make more informed decisions about their academic and career choices, ultimately leading to greater job satisfaction and fulfillment.

Overall, self-assessment tools are powerful resources for students looking to develop their marketable skills and succeed in the job market. By taking the time to reflect on their personality traits, strengths, and interests, students can gain valuable insights into themselves and make informed decisions about their career paths. Whether it's through the MBTI, StrengthsFinder, or interest inventories, these tools can help students unlock their full potential and achieve their professional goals.

Identifying Transferable Skills

Identifying transferable skills is a crucial step in developing a successful career path. These skills are abilities that can be applied across various jobs and industries, making them highly valuable in today's competitive job market. As students, it is important to recognize and cultivate these skills to increase our marketability and stand out to potential employers.

One way to identify transferable skills is to reflect on past experiences, both in and out of the classroom. For example, if you have worked on group projects or volunteered for a community organization, you may have developed skills such as teamwork, communication, and problem-solving. These skills are highly transferable and can be applied to a wide range of jobs, from customer service to project management.

Another way to identify transferable skills is to assess your strengths and weaknesses. Consider what tasks or activities you excel at and what areas you may need to improve upon. By understanding your strengths, you can better leverage them in your job search and highlight them to potential employers. Likewise, by working on your weaknesses, you can further develop your skill set and become a more well-rounded candidate.

It is also helpful to seek feedback from others, such as professors, mentors, or peers. They may have insights into your strengths and weaknesses that you may not have considered. Additionally, they can provide guidance on how to further develop your transferable skills and make yourself more marketable to employers.

In conclusion, identifying transferable skills is essential for students looking to navigate the job market and develop marketable skills. By reflecting on past experiences, assessing strengths and weaknesses, and seeking feedback from others, students can better understand their skill set and leverage it to stand out to potential employers. Developing transferable skills is an ongoing process, but with dedication and effort, students can increase their marketability and achieve success in their chosen career paths.

Exploring Career Paths

One of the most important steps in developing marketable skills is exploring different career paths. As students, it can be easy to feel overwhelmed by the many options available, but taking the time to research and consider different industries and professions can help you make informed decisions about your future. By exploring different career paths, you can gain a better understanding of the skills and qualifications needed for various roles, as well as the potential job opportunities and salary ranges.

One way to explore career paths is by conducting informational interviews with professionals in fields that interest you. Informational interviews give you the opportunity to learn more about a specific industry or job role from someone who is already working in that field. By asking questions about their day-to-day responsibilities, career progression, and challenges they face, you can gain valuable insights into what it takes to succeed in that particular career path.

Another way to explore career paths is by participating in internships or job shadowing opportunities. These experiences allow you to gain hands-on experience in a specific industry or job role, giving you a firsthand look at what it's like to work in that field. By getting a taste of different career paths through internships or job shadowing, you can better assess your interests and strengths, and determine which career paths align best with your goals and aspirations.

     Networking is also a key component of exploring career paths. By connecting with professionals in different industries through networking events, career fairs, and online platforms like LinkedIn, you can learn more about different career paths and gain valuable insights and advice from those who are already established in their careers. Networking can also help you uncover hidden job opportunities and build relationships with potential mentors who can guide you in your career development.

     Exploring career paths is an essential step in developing marketable skills as a student. By conducting informational interviews, participating in internships or job shadowing opportunities, and networking with professionals in different industries, you can gain valuable insights into the various career paths available to you. Taking the time to explore different career paths will help you make informed decisions about your future and set yourself up for success in a competitive job market.

Chapter 4: Developing Marketable Skills

Acquiring Industry-Relevant Certifications

In today's competitive job market, it is essential for students to acquire industry-relevant certifications to stand out from the crowd. These certifications can demonstrate to potential employers that you have the necessary skills and knowledge to succeed in a particular field. By obtaining these certifications, you can increase your chances of landing a job and advancing your career.

One of the most popular industry-relevant certifications is the Project Management Professional (PMP) certification. This certification is recognized globally and demonstrates that you have the skills and knowledge to lead and manage projects effectively. By obtaining a PMP certification, you can show potential employers that you have what it takes to successfully navigate complex projects and deliver results on time and within budget.

Another valuable industry-relevant certification is the Certified Information Systems Security Professional (CISSP) certification. This certification is ideal for students interested in pursuing a career in cybersecurity. By obtaining a CISSP certification, you can demonstrate to employers that you have the expertise to protect organizations from cyber threats and safeguard sensitive information.

In addition to the PMP and CISSP certifications, there are numerous other industry-relevant certifications available in fields such as marketing, healthcare, finance, and technology. By researching the certifications that are most relevant to your desired career path, you can identify opportunities to enhance your skills and make yourself more marketable to potential employers.

Overall, acquiring industry-relevant certifications is a valuable investment in your future career success. By obtaining these certifications, you can demonstrate your expertise and dedication to your field, which can help you stand out in a competitive job market. Take the time to research the certifications that are most relevant to your career goals and start building your credentials today.

Building Technical Skills

In today's competitive job market, having strong technical skills is essential for standing out to potential employers. Technical skills are specific abilities that are related to a particular job or industry, such as programming languages, software proficiency, or data analysis. Developing these skills can greatly increase your marketability and open up more opportunities for you in your desired field.

One of the best ways to build technical skills is through hands-on experience. This can include internships, co-op programs, or volunteer work that allow you to apply your skills in a real-world setting. By gaining practical experience, you can learn how to navigate challenges and solve problems that you may not encounter in a classroom setting. Additionally, working with professionals in the field can provide valuable mentorship and networking opportunities that can help you advance in your career.

Another way to build technical skills is through online courses and certifications. There are a plethora of resources available online that can help you learn new skills or enhance existing ones. Websites like Coursera, Udemy, and LinkedIn Learning offer courses in a wide range of technical topics, from coding to graphic design to project management. By taking advantage of these resources, you can stay current with industry trends and demonstrate your commitment to continuous learning.

Networking with professionals in your desired field can also help you build technical skills. Attend industry events, join professional organizations, or connect with alumni who are working in your field. By building relationships with experienced professionals, you can gain insights into the skills that are most valued in the industry and learn about new opportunities for growth and development. Additionally, networking can help you build a support system of like-minded individuals who can provide guidance and advice as you navigate your career.

Ultimately, building technical skills is an ongoing process that requires dedication and perseverance. By seeking out opportunities for hands-on experience, taking online courses, and networking with professionals in your field, you can develop the skills that will set you apart in the job market. Remember that building technical skills is not just about adding bullet points to your resume – it's about equipping yourself with the knowledge and abilities needed to excel in your chosen career path.

Enhancing Soft Skills

In today's competitive job market, having strong technical skills is no longer enough to stand out to potential employers. Soft skills, such as communication, teamwork, and problem-solving abilities, are becoming increasingly important in the workplace. In this subchapter, we will explore the importance of enhancing soft skills and how students can develop and showcase these valuable abilities to prospective employers.

One key soft skill that is highly sought after by employers is communication. Being able to effectively communicate with colleagues, clients, and supervisors is essential for success in any job. Students can enhance their communication skills by actively listening, asking thoughtful questions, and practicing clear and concise writing. Participating in group projects, presentations, and public speaking events can also help students build confidence in their communication abilities.

Another important soft skill is teamwork. Employers value employees who can collaborate effectively with others to achieve common goals. Students can develop their teamwork skills by participating in group projects, extracurricular activities, and volunteer work. Learning how to compromise, delegate tasks, and support team members can help students become valuable team players in the workplace.

Problem-solving skills are also highly prized by employers. Being able to think critically, analyze information, and propose creative solutions to challenges is a valuable asset in any job. Students can enhance their problem-solving abilities by tackling complex assignments, participating in case studies, and seeking out opportunities to apply their knowledge in real-world situations. Developing a growth mindset and being open to learning from failures can also help students become more effective problem solvers.

In addition to communication, teamwork, and problem-solving skills, other soft skills that students should focus on developing include adaptability, time management, and emotional intelligence. Employers are looking for candidates who can navigate change, prioritize tasks, and manage their emotions in high-pressure situations. By honing these soft skills, students can increase their marketability and stand out to potential employers in a crowded job market. Overall, enhancing soft skills is essential for students looking to succeed in their careers and make a positive impact in the workplace.

Chapter 5: Gaining Practical Experience

Internships and Co-op Opportunities

Internships and co-op opportunities are invaluable experiences for students looking to develop their marketable skills and gain real-world experience in their chosen field. These opportunities allow students to apply the knowledge they have gained in the classroom to practical, hands-on situations, giving them a competitive edge in the job market.

One of the key benefits of internships and co-op opportunities is the chance to network with professionals in the industry. Building relationships with potential employers can open doors to future job opportunities and provide valuable insights into the industry. By making a positive impression during an internship or co-op, students can increase their chances of securing a full-time job after graduation.

Additionally, internships and co-op opportunities provide students with the opportunity to test out different career paths and industries before committing to a specific career. This hands-on experience can help students determine if a particular field is the right fit for them and can help them narrow down their career options. This exploration can be invaluable in helping students make informed decisions about their future career paths.

Internships and co-op opportunities also allow students to develop essential skills that are highly sought after by employers. By working in a professional setting, students can improve their communication, teamwork, problem-solving, and time management skills. These skills are transferable to any career and can give students a competitive edge in the job market.

In conclusion, internships and co-op opportunities are essential for students looking to develop their marketable skills and gain valuable experience in their chosen field. By taking advantage of these opportunities, students can build relationships with industry professionals, explore different career paths, and develop essential skills that will make them stand out to potential employers. Students should actively seek out internships and co-op opportunities to enhance their academic learning and prepare themselves for a successful career in the future.

Volunteer Work and Extracurricular Activities

Volunteer work and extracurricular activities are valuable experiences that can help students develop important skills that are highly marketable in today's job market. By engaging in volunteer work, students have the opportunity to give back to their communities while also gaining hands-on experience in a variety of areas. Whether it's volunteering at a local non-profit organization, participating in a service trip, or helping out at a school event, students can learn valuable skills such as teamwork, leadership, communication, and problem-solving.

Extracurricular activities, such as joining clubs and sports teams, can also help students develop marketable skills. By participating in these activities, students have the chance to hone their time management and organizational skills, as well as build relationships and network with others who share similar interests. Additionally, extracurricular activities can provide students with leadership opportunities, allowing them to take on roles such as team captain or club president, which can showcase their ability to lead and motivate others.

Employers often look for candidates who have a well-rounded skill set, and volunteer work and extracurricular activities can help students stand out from the competition. These experiences demonstrate to employers that students are motivated, proactive, and have a strong work ethic. By showcasing their involvement in volunteer work and extracurricular activities on their resumes and during job interviews, students can highlight their ability to take initiative, work well with others, and contribute positively to their communities.

In addition to developing marketable skills, volunteer work and extracurricular activities can also help students explore their interests and passions, and discover potential career paths. By engaging in different activities, students can gain a better understanding of their strengths and weaknesses, as well as what they enjoy doing. This self-awareness can be valuable when it comes to choosing a career path and pursuing opportunities that align with their interests and goals.

In conclusion, volunteer work and extracurricular activities are essential components of developing marketable skills that can help students succeed in the job market. By actively participating in these activities, students can gain valuable experience, develop important skills, and showcase their strengths to potential employers. Ultimately, engaging in volunteer work and extracurricular activities can not only enhance students' resumes and job prospects, but also provide them with personal and professional growth opportunities that will benefit them in the long run.

Networking and Mentorship

Networking and mentorship are two crucial components in developing marketable skills as a student. Networking involves building relationships with professionals in your field of interest, while mentorship entails seeking guidance and advice from experienced individuals who can help you navigate the complexities of the job market. Both networking and mentorship can provide invaluable insights and opportunities that can help you stand out among your peers and secure desirable job opportunities.

One of the key benefits of networking is the opportunity to connect with professionals who can provide valuable advice and insights into the industry. By attending networking events, joining professional organizations, and reaching out to professionals on platforms like LinkedIn, students can expand their professional network and gain access to valuable resources and opportunities. Networking also allows students to learn about the latest trends and developments in their field, which can help them stay ahead of the curve and develop the skills that are in demand by employers.

Mentorship is another important aspect of developing marketable skills as a student. A mentor can provide guidance, support, and encouragement as you navigate the job market and work towards achieving your career goals. A mentor can offer valuable insights into the industry, help you identify your strengths and weaknesses, and provide constructive feedback to help you improve your skills. Additionally, a mentor can help you expand your professional network by introducing you to other professionals in the field and recommending you for job opportunities.

When seeking out mentors, students should look for individuals who have experience and expertise in their field of interest, as well as a willingness to invest time and effort in their development. A good mentor is someone who is supportive, knowledgeable, and willing to share their experiences and insights with you. By building strong relationships with mentors, students can gain access to valuable advice, resources, and opportunities that can help them develop the skills and experience needed to succeed in the job market.

In conclusion, networking and mentorship are essential components of developing marketable skills as a student. By actively networking with professionals in their field and seeking out mentors who can provide guidance and support, students can gain valuable insights, opportunities, and resources that can help them stand out in a competitive job market. Networking and mentorship can help students build relationships, expand their professional network, and gain access to valuable advice and support that can help them achieve their career goals. By prioritizing networking and mentorship, students can develop the skills and experience needed to succeed in their chosen field and secure desirable job opportunities.

Chapter 6: Showcasing Your Skills to Employers

Building a Strong Resume

Building a strong resume is crucial for students looking to stand out in today's competitive job market. Your resume is often the first impression a potential employer will have of you, so it's important to make sure it effectively showcases your skills and experiences. In this subchapter, we will discuss the key components of a strong resume and provide tips on how to make yours stand out.

When building your resume, it's important to include relevant skills and experiences that align with the job you are applying for. Start by creating a master resume that includes all of your experiences, then tailor it to each job you apply for by highlighting the skills and experiences that are most relevant to the position. This will show employers that you have the skills they are looking for and are a good fit for the role.

In addition to highlighting your skills and experiences, it's important to make sure your resume is well-organized and easy to read. Use clear headings and bullet points to make the information easy to digest. A clean, professional-looking resume will make a good impression on employers and show that you are detail-oriented and organized.

Another key component of a strong resume is a well-written summary or objective statement at the top. This should briefly summarize your skills and experiences and explain why you are a good fit for the position. This will give employers a quick overview of your qualifications and make them want to learn more about you.

Finally, don't forget to proofread your resume carefully before submitting it. Typos and grammatical errors can make a bad impression on employers and make you appear careless. Take the time to review your resume multiple times and consider asking a friend or mentor to review it as well. A strong resume can be the key to landing your dream job, so make sure yours is polished and professional.

Crafting a Compelling Cover Letter

Crafting a compelling cover letter is an essential skill for students looking to enter the job market and develop their marketable skills. Your cover letter is often the first impression you make on a potential employer, so it's important to make it stand out. In this subchapter, we will provide you with tips and strategies to help you create a cover letter that will capture the attention of hiring managers and showcase your skills and qualifications.

When crafting a cover letter, it's important to personalize it for each job application. Avoid using generic templates and instead tailor your cover letter to the specific job and company you are applying to. Start by researching the company and understanding their values, mission, and culture. Use this information to demonstrate how your skills and experience align with what the company is looking for in a candidate.

In your cover letter, highlight your most relevant skills and experiences that make you a strong candidate for the position. Use specific examples to demonstrate how you have successfully applied these skills in the past. Avoid simply restating your resume – instead, use your cover letter to provide more context and depth to your qualifications.

In addition to showcasing your skills and experiences, your cover letter should also convey your enthusiasm and passion for the role. Employers are looking for candidates who are genuinely interested in the job and the company, so make sure to express your excitement about the opportunity. Show that you have done your homework and understand how this position fits into your career goals.

Finally, make sure to proofread your cover letter carefully before submitting it. Spelling and grammar errors can make a negative impression on hiring managers, so take the time to review your cover letter for any mistakes. Additionally, consider asking a mentor, career counselor, or friend to review your cover letter and provide feedback. With a well-crafted cover letter, you can effectively showcase your skills and qualifications and increase your chances of landing your dream job.

Creating an Impressive Portfolio

Creating an impressive portfolio is essential for students looking to stand out in today's competitive job market. A portfolio is a collection of your best work that showcases your skills, experiences, and accomplishments. It is a powerful tool that allows you to demonstrate your abilities to potential employers and differentiate yourself from other candidates.

To create an impressive portfolio, start by gathering samples of your work that highlight your skills and accomplishments. This can include projects, papers, presentations, and any other work that demonstrates your abilities. Make sure to choose examples that are relevant to the types of jobs you are applying for and that showcase your strengths.

Once you have gathered your work samples, organize them in a professional and visually appealing way. Consider creating an online portfolio using platforms like LinkedIn, Behance, or a personal website. Make sure to include a brief description of each piece of work, explaining the skills and experiences you gained from it.

In addition to showcasing your work, your portfolio should also include a resume and a cover letter. These documents should be tailored to the specific job you are applying for and highlight your relevant skills and experiences. Make sure to proofread and edit these documents carefully to ensure they are error-free and professional.

Finally, regularly update and refine your portfolio as you gain new skills and experiences. Keep track of your accomplishments and add them to your portfolio to constantly improve and showcase your abilities. By creating an impressive portfolio, you will be able to effectively market yourself to potential employers and increase your chances of landing your dream job in today's competitive job market.

Chapter 7: Navigating the Job Search Process

Job Search Strategies

In today's competitive job market, it is essential for students to develop effective job search strategies in order to land their dream job. This subchapter will explore various strategies that students can use to navigate the job market and secure employment in their desired field. By implementing these strategies, students can increase their chances of success and stand out to potential employers.

One important job search strategy is networking. Building relationships with professionals in your desired industry can open up new opportunities and give you access to valuable resources. Attend networking events, join professional organizations, and connect with alumni from your school to expand your network. By cultivating these relationships, you can gain insights into the job market, receive valuable advice, and potentially uncover hidden job opportunities.

Another key strategy is to tailor your resume and cover letter to each job application. Customize your application materials to highlight your relevant skills and experiences that align with the job requirements. This shows potential employers that you have taken the time to research the position and are genuinely interested in the role. Additionally, make sure to proofread your materials carefully to avoid any typos or grammatical errors that could detract from your professionalism.

Utilizing online job boards and career websites is another effective strategy for finding job opportunities. Websites such as Indeed, LinkedIn, and Glassdoor allow you to search for jobs based on your desired criteria, such as location, industry, and job title. Set up job alerts to receive notifications when new positions are posted that match your preferences. Remember to regularly update your profile and resume on these platforms to increase your visibility to recruiters.

In addition to traditional job search methods, consider exploring alternative pathways to employment, such as internships, freelance work, or volunteer opportunities. These experiences can help you gain valuable skills, build your professional network, and enhance your resume. Be open to different types of opportunities that may not be your ideal job but can serve as stepping stones to your ultimate career goals. By being flexible and proactive in your job search, you can increase your chances of finding a fulfilling and rewarding career

Interview Preparation

Interview preparation is a crucial step in the job search process. It is your opportunity to showcase your skills and experiences to potential employers and make a strong impression. To ensure you are well-prepared for your interviews, there are several steps you can take.

First, research the company where you will be interviewing. Learn about its mission, values, and culture. This will not only help you understand if the company is a good fit for you, but it will also show the interviewer that you are genuinely interested in the position.

Next, practice your responses to common interview questions. Think about your strengths, weaknesses, and examples of how you have demonstrated key skills in past experiences. By practicing your answers, you will be able to articulate your thoughts clearly and confidently during the interview.

It is also important to dress appropriately for the interview. Your appearance can make a big impact on the interviewer's first impression of you. Dress in professional attire that is suitable for the company's dress code.

During the interview, be sure to ask questions about the company and the position. This shows that you are engaged and interested in learning more about the organization. It also provides you with valuable information to determine if the job is the right fit for you.

Finally, follow up with a thank you note after the interview. Express your appreciation for the opportunity to interview and reiterate your interest in the position. This gesture can leave a positive impression on the interviewer and set you apart from other candidates. By following these steps, you can ensure that you are well-prepared for your interviews and increase your chances of landing your dream job.

Negotiating Job Offers

Negotiating job offers can be a nerve-wracking experience for many students entering the job market. However, it is an essential skill to develop in order to secure the best possible opportunities for yourself. When negotiating a job offer, it is important to remember that you are not just accepting a salary, but also negotiating for benefits, work-life balance, and career growth opportunities.

One key tip for negotiating a job offer is to do your research. Before entering into negotiations, make sure you have a clear understanding of the market value for your skills and experience. This will give you a solid foundation to negotiate from and help you make informed decisions about what is fair and reasonable.

Another important aspect of negotiating a job offer is to be confident in your worth. Remember that the company has already expressed interest in hiring you, so you have leverage in the negotiation process. Be prepared to articulate your value to the company and why you are worth the salary and benefits you are asking for.

It is also important to be flexible in your negotiations. While it is important to advocate for yourself and what you believe you deserve, it is also important to be open to compromise. Consider what is most important to you in a job offer and be willing to make concessions in other areas if necessary.

Finally, always remember to negotiate in a professional and respectful manner. Be clear and direct in your communication, but also be willing to listen and consider the perspective of the employer. By approaching negotiations with a positive and collaborative attitude, you can increase your chances of securing a job offer that meets your needs and sets you up for success in your career.

Chapter 8: Continuous Learning and Skill Development

Lifelong Learning Opportunities

In today's rapidly changing job market, it has become essential for students to embrace lifelong learning opportunities in order to stay competitive and develop marketable skills. Lifelong learning refers to the continuous process of acquiring new knowledge and skills throughout one's life, beyond the traditional classroom setting. By actively seeking out opportunities to learn and grow, students can enhance their employability and adaptability in the ever-evolving job market.

One of the most valuable lifelong learning opportunities for students is gaining real-world experience through internships, co-op programs, and part-time jobs. These hands-on experiences not only provide students with practical skills and industry knowledge but also help them build a professional network and gain insights into different career paths. By taking advantage of these opportunities, students can develop a competitive edge and stand out to potential employers.

Another important aspect of lifelong learning is staying informed about industry trends and advancements. This can be achieved through attending conferences, workshops, webinars, and networking events related to one's field of interest. By staying up-to-date with the latest developments in their industry, students can demonstrate their commitment to continuous learning and show employers that they are proactive and forward-thinking.

Furthermore, seeking out mentorship and guidance from industry professionals can also be a valuable lifelong learning opportunity for students. Mentors can provide valuable insights, advice, and support to help students navigate their career paths and make informed decisions. By building relationships with mentors, students can gain valuable feedback, learn from their experiences, and expand their professional network.

Embracing lifelong learning opportunities is essential for students looking to develop marketable skills and succeed in the competitive job market. By gaining real-world experience, staying informed about industry trends, and seeking mentorship, students can enhance their employability, adaptability, and overall career prospects. It is important for students to take initiative and actively pursue opportunities for learning and growth throughout their academic and professional journey.

Professional Development Resources

In today's competitive job market, it is essential for students to constantly seek out professional development resources in order to stay ahead of the curve and increase their marketability. By actively engaging in skill-building activities and seeking out opportunities for growth, students can enhance their chances of securing their dream job after graduation. This subchapter will explore some of the key professional development resources available to students looking to develop their marketable skills.

One valuable resource for students seeking to enhance their marketable skills is career counseling services offered by their college or university. Career counselors can provide students with personalized guidance on how to identify their strengths and weaknesses, set career goals, and develop a plan for achieving them. They can also offer assistance with resume writing, interview preparation, and networking strategies, all of which are essential skills for success in the job market.

Another important professional development resource for students is internships and co-op programs. These opportunities allow students to gain real-world experience in their chosen field, build their professional network, and develop valuable skills that will make them more attractive to potential employers. By participating in internships and co-ops, students can also test out different career paths and gain insight into what type of work environment and role best suits their interests and strengths.

Online learning platforms such as Coursera, Udemy, and LinkedIn Learning are also valuable resources for students looking to develop their marketable skills. These platforms offer a wide range of courses on topics such as coding, digital marketing, project management, and more, allowing students to learn new skills at their own pace and on their own schedule. By taking advantage of these online learning opportunities, students can expand their knowledge base, enhance their skill set, and make themselves more attractive to potential employers.

Networking events, career fairs, and industry conferences are additional professional development resources that can help students expand their professional network, learn about job opportunities, and gain insight into industry trends. By attending these events, students can connect with professionals in their field, learn from experts, and gain valuable insights that can help them advance their career. Building a strong professional network is essential in today's job market, and these events provide valuable opportunities for students to make connections and build relationships that can help them succeed in their chosen field. By actively seeking out and engaging with these professional development resources, students can enhance their marketable skills, stand out to potential employers, and increase their chances of landing their dream job after graduation.

Staying Relevant in a Changing Job Market

In today's rapidly evolving job market, it is more important than ever for students to stay relevant and competitive. With advancements in technology and changes in industry trends, the skills that employers are looking for are constantly shifting. As such, it is crucial for students to develop and maintain marketable skills that will set them apart from the competition.

One way to stay relevant in a changing job market is to continually update and expand your skill set. This may involve taking courses, attending workshops, or obtaining certifications in areas that are in high demand. By staying current with the latest industry trends and technologies, you can position yourself as a valuable asset to potential employers.

Networking is another key component of staying relevant in today's job market. Building relationships with professionals in your field can open up new opportunities and help you stay informed about the latest developments in your industry. Attend networking events, join professional organizations, and connect with alumni to expand your network and stay plugged in to the job market.

Adaptability is also essential for staying relevant in a changing job market. As industries evolve and new technologies emerge, it is important to be flexible and willing to learn new skills. Being open to change and willing to adapt to new circumstances will make you more attractive to employers and increase your chances of success in a competitive job market.

Finally, it is important for students to stay proactive in their career development. Take initiative in seeking out new opportunities for growth and advancement, and don't be afraid to step out of your comfort zone. By continuously seeking ways to improve and grow, you can ensure that you remain relevant in the ever-changing job market and position yourself for long-term success in your career.

Chapter 9: Overcoming Challenges in the Job Market

Dealing with Rejection

Dealing with rejection is an inevitable part of the job search process. As students navigating the job market, it's important to understand that rejection is not a reflection of your worth or abilities. Instead, it's an opportunity for growth and self-improvement. Learning how to handle rejection in a positive and constructive manner can help you develop valuable skills that will benefit you throughout your career.

One of the first steps in dealing with rejection is to not take it personally. Remember that job hunting is a competitive process, and there are often many qualified candidates vying for the same position. It's important to separate your personal identity from the rejection and understand that it's simply a part of the job search process. By reframing rejection as a learning experience rather than a personal failure, you can maintain a positive attitude and continue to pursue your career goals.

Another important aspect of dealing with rejection is to seek feedback whenever possible. While it can be difficult to hear criticism, feedback from employers can provide valuable insights into areas where you can improve. Whether it's through a formal rejection email or a follow-up phone call, don't be afraid to ask for feedback on your application or interview performance. Use this feedback as a learning opportunity to refine your skills and make yourself a more competitive candidate in the future.

In addition to seeking feedback, it's important to stay resilient and persistent in the face of rejection. Job hunting can be a long and challenging process, and it's easy to become discouraged after facing multiple rejections. However, it's important to remember that every rejection brings you one step closer to finding the right opportunity. Stay focused on your goals, continue to network and apply for new positions, and don't let rejection deter you from pursuing your dreams.

Finally, remember that rejection is not the end of the road. It's simply a detour on your journey to finding the right job. Use each rejection as an opportunity to reflect on your strengths and weaknesses, refine your job search strategy, and continue to develop your marketable skills. By approaching rejection with resilience, a positive attitude, and a willingness to learn and grow, you'll be better equipped to navigate the job market and ultimately land the job that's right for you.

Addressing Skill Gaps

Addressing skill gaps is a crucial step in ensuring success in today's competitive job market. As students, it is important to identify and work on developing the skills that are most in demand by employers. By addressing skill gaps early on in your academic career, you can position yourself as a strong candidate for internships and entry-level positions upon graduation.

One way to address skill gaps is to take advantage of the resources available to you on your college campus. Many schools offer career services that can help you identify areas where you may be lacking in skills and provide you with opportunities to develop those skills. Whether it's through workshops, career fairs, or one-on-one counseling, these resources can be invaluable in helping you bridge the gap between your current skills and the skills required by employers in your desired field.

Another way to address skill gaps is to seek out internships or part-time jobs that will allow you to gain hands-on experience in your chosen field. These opportunities not only provide you with valuable real-world experience, but they also give you the chance to develop and hone the skills that are most in demand by employers. By taking on internships or part-time jobs, you can demonstrate to potential employers that you are proactive and willing to put in the work to develop the skills necessary for success in your chosen field.

In addition to seeking out internships and part-time jobs, you can also address skill gaps by taking advantage of online resources and courses. Many websites offer free or low-cost courses in a wide range of subjects, from data analysis to graphic design to project management. By taking these courses, you can gain valuable skills that will make you a more attractive candidate to employers in your desired field.

Ultimately, addressing skill gaps is a proactive and ongoing process that requires dedication and hard work. By identifying areas where you may be lacking in skills, seeking out opportunities to develop those skills, and taking advantage of the resources available to you, you can position yourself for success in the job market and stand out as a strong candidate to potential employers.

Managing Career Transitions

Managing career transitions can be a challenging but necessary part of building a successful career. As students, it is important to be prepared for the inevitable changes that will come as you navigate the job market.

Whether you are transitioning from one job to another, moving to a new city for a job opportunity, or changing career paths entirely, having a plan in place can help ease the transition and set you up for success.

One key aspect of managing career transitions is developing and honing your marketable skills. These are the skills that make you stand out to potential employers and help you excel in your chosen field. By continually improving and expanding your skill set, you can adapt to new roles and opportunities with confidence. Take the time to assess your current skills and identify areas where you can improve or learn new skills that are in demand in your industry.

Networking is another crucial component of managing career transitions. Building and maintaining a strong professional network can open doors to new opportunities and help you navigate transitions more smoothly. Attend networking events, connect with professionals in your field on LinkedIn, and reach out to alumni or mentors for advice and support. By cultivating relationships with others in your industry, you can stay informed about job openings, gain insights into different career paths, and receive valuable guidance as you navigate career transitions.

It is also important to stay flexible and open-minded when managing career transitions. The job market is constantly evolving, and new opportunities may arise that you had not considered before. Be willing to explore different career paths, take on new challenges, and step outside of your comfort zone. By remaining open to new possibilities, you can discover exciting opportunities that align with your skills and interests, and ultimately lead to a fulfilling and successful career.

Finally, remember that managing career transitions is a process that takes time and effort. Be patient with yourself as you navigate the ups and downs of the job market, and seek out resources and support to help you along the way. Whether it's career counseling, resume workshops, or networking events, there are many resources available to help you succeed in managing career transitions. By taking proactive steps to develop your marketable skills, build a strong network, stay flexible and open-minded, and seek out support when needed, you can confidently navigate career transitions and build a successful and rewarding career.

Chapter 10: Success Stories and Advice from Industry Professionals

Insights from Successful Professionals

In this subchapter, we will explore the valuable advice and experiences shared by professionals who have successfully navigated the job market and developed highly marketable skills. These insights will provide students with valuable lessons and strategies to help them thrive in their own career journeys.

One common theme that emerges from the advice of successful professionals is the importance of continuous learning and skill development. Many professionals emphasize the value of seeking out opportunities for growth and improvement, whether through formal education, online courses, or hands-on experience. By constantly expanding their skill sets and staying abreast of industry trends, these professionals have been able to adapt to the evolving job market and remain competitive in their fields.

Another key insight shared by successful professionals is the importance of networking and building relationships within their industries. By connecting with colleagues, mentors, and industry leaders, these professionals have been able to access valuable resources, opportunities, and support systems that have propelled their careers forward. Networking is a valuable skill that can open doors to new job opportunities, collaborations, and professional development initiatives.

Additionally, successful professionals stress the importance of setting clear goals and creating a roadmap for their career paths. By outlining their short-term and long-term objectives, these professionals have been able to stay focused and motivated in pursuing their professional aspirations. Setting achievable goals and regularly assessing progress towards them can help students develop a clear sense of direction and purpose in their own career journeys.

Successful professionals encourage students to embrace failure as a learning opportunity and to persevere in the face of setbacks. Many professionals acknowledge that failure is a natural part of the learning process and that resilience and perseverance are key traits that have helped them overcome challenges and achieve success in their careers. By cultivating a growth mindset and viewing failures as opportunities for growth and self-improvement, students can develop the resilience and determination needed to navigate the job market and develop highly marketable skills.

Tips for Career Advancement

In today's competitive job market, it is essential for students to develop marketable skills that will set them apart from other candidates and help them advance in their careers. Whether you are a recent graduate looking for your first job or a seasoned professional seeking to move up the corporate ladder, there are several key tips for career advancement that can help you achieve your goals.

One important tip for career advancement is to continuously seek out opportunities for learning and skill development. This could involve enrolling in online courses, attending workshops and seminars, or pursuing certifications in your field. By staying current with industry trends and expanding your knowledge base, you will be better equipped to take on new challenges and responsibilities in your career.

Another tip for career advancement is to build a strong professional network. Networking can open doors to new job opportunities, mentorship relationships, and valuable connections within your industry. Attend industry events, join professional organizations, and connect with colleagues on platforms like LinkedIn to expand your network and increase your visibility in your field.

It is also important to set clear goals for your career advancement and create a plan to achieve them. This could involve setting short-term and long-term goals, identifying the steps needed to reach them, and regularly assessing your progress. By having a clear roadmap for your career development, you will be better able to stay focused and motivated as you work towards your goals.

Additionally, it is crucial to showcase your skills and accomplishments to potential employers or supervisors. This could involve updating your resume and LinkedIn profile, creating a portfolio of your work, or proactively seeking out opportunities to demonstrate your skills. By effectively communicating your value to others, you will increase your chances of being recognized and rewarded for your contributions in your career.

Finally, remember to stay adaptable and open to new opportunities in your career advancement journey. The job market is constantly evolving, and the skills that are in demand today may not be as relevant tomorrow. By staying flexible and willing to learn new skills, you will be better positioned to navigate changes in your industry and seize opportunities for growth and advancement in your career.

Lessons Learned from Real-World Experiences

In this chapter, students will gain valuable insights from individuals who have successfully navigated the job market and developed marketable skills. These real-world experiences serve as powerful examples of the importance of honing one's skills and adapting to the ever-changing demands of the workforce. By learning from the experiences of others, students can better prepare themselves for the challenges and opportunities that lie ahead in their careers.

One key lesson that students can take away from real-world experiences is the importance of continuous learning and skill development. The job market is constantly evolving, and it is essential for individuals to stay ahead of the curve by acquiring new skills and knowledge. By investing in their own personal and professional development, students can position themselves as valuable assets to potential employers and increase their chances of success in the job market.

Another valuable lesson from real-world experiences is the importance of networking and building relationships. Many successful professionals attribute their career advancement to the connections they have made along the way. By actively networking and cultivating relationships with industry professionals, students can open up new opportunities for themselves and gain valuable insights into their chosen field. Building a strong network can also provide students with the support and guidance they need to navigate the challenges of the job market.

Additionally, real-world experiences can teach students the importance of adaptability and resilience in the face of adversity. The job market is unpredictable, and individuals may encounter setbacks and obstacles along the way. By learning how to adapt to changing circumstances and bounce back from failure, students can develop the resilience needed to overcome challenges and achieve their goals. Through real-world experiences, students can gain a deeper understanding of the importance of perseverance and determination in their career journey.

Overall, the lessons learned from real-world experiences can provide students with valuable insights and guidance as they navigate the job market and develop marketable skills. By learning from the experiences of others, students can better prepare themselves for the challenges and opportunities that lie ahead in their careers. By investing in continuous learning, building strong relationships, and developing resilience, students can position themselves for success in the competitive job market.

Chapter 11: Conclusion

Recap of Key Points

In this subchapter, we will recap some of the key points discussed in the book "Navigating the Job Market: How Students Can Develop Marketable Skills." As students, it is important to understand the significance of developing marketable skills to stand out in today's competitive job market. By honing these skills, you can increase your chances of securing a fulfilling and successful career.

One of the key points emphasized in this book is the importance of identifying your strengths and interests. Take the time to assess your skills, talents, and passions to determine what sets you apart from other candidates. By understanding what makes you unique, you can better tailor your job search and focus on opportunities that align with your strengths.

Another important point to remember is the value of gaining experience through internships, part-time jobs, and volunteer work. Employers are looking for candidates who have practical experience in their field, so it is crucial to seek out opportunities to build your resume. These experiences will not only help you develop new skills but also demonstrate your commitment and dedication to potential employers.

Networking is another key point discussed in this book. Building connections with professionals in your desired industry can open up doors to new opportunities and provide valuable insights into the job market. Attend networking events, join professional organizations, and reach out to alumni or mentors for guidance and support as you navigate your career path.

Lastly, never stop learning and growing. The job market is constantly evolving, and it is important to stay current with industry trends and developments. Take advantage of professional development opportunities, workshops, and online courses to enhance your skills and stay competitive in your field. By continuously investing in your personal and professional growth, you can position yourself for long-term success in the job market.

Final Thoughts and Action Steps

In this final section of the book, we want to leave you with some key takeaways and action steps to help you navigate the job market successfully and develop the marketable skills that employers are looking for. As students, it's important to recognize that the job market is competitive, and you need to set yourself apart from the crowd. By developing marketable skills, you can increase your chances of landing a job that aligns with your interests and goals.

First and foremost, it's essential to identify your strengths and weaknesses. Take the time to assess your skills and abilities, and determine where you excel and where you could use improvement. This self-awareness will help you focus on developing the marketable skills that will make you a valuable asset to potential employers. Whether it's technical skills, communication skills, or leadership abilities, honing in on your strengths will set you up for success in the job market.

Next, consider seeking out opportunities for experiential learning. Internships, volunteer work, part-time jobs, and extracurricular activities can all provide valuable hands-on experience that will help you develop marketable skills. These opportunities will not only enhance your resume but also allow you to test out different career paths and industries to see what fits best for you. Remember, the more experience you have, the more marketable you will be to employers.

Networking is another crucial aspect of navigating the job market and developing marketable skills. Building relationships with professionals in your desired field can open doors to new opportunities and help you stay informed about industry trends and job openings. Attend networking events, connect with alumni, and reach out to professionals for informational interviews. By expanding your network, you increase your chances of finding a job that aligns with your skills and interests.

Lastly, don't be afraid to continue learning and growing. The job market is constantly evolving, and it's essential to stay current with industry trends and advancements. Take advantage of professional development opportunities, online courses, and workshops to enhance your skills and knowledge. By demonstrating a commitment to lifelong learning, you show employers that you are adaptable, motivated, and dedicated to your personal and professional growth. Remember, developing marketable skills is an ongoing process, and by taking proactive steps to improve yourself, you increase your chances of success in the job market.

Resources for Further Exploration

In order to truly excel in the job market, it is essential for students to continue developing their marketable skills even after they have completed their formal education. This subchapter, titled "Resources for Further Exploration," is designed to provide students with a comprehensive list of resources that can help them continue to grow and develop their skills in a variety of areas.

One valuable resource that students can utilize is online courses and tutorials. Platforms such as Coursera, Udemy, and LinkedIn Learning offer a wide range of courses on topics such as coding, digital marketing, project management, and more. These courses are often taught by industry experts and can provide students with hands-on experience and practical skills that are highly sought after by employers.

Another valuable resource for students looking to develop their marketable skills is professional organizations and networking groups. Joining groups related to their field of interest can provide students with access to valuable resources, networking opportunities, and mentorship from seasoned professionals. These groups often offer workshops, seminars, and networking events that can help students stay current in their field and make valuable connections.

Career fairs and job expos are also excellent resources for students looking to explore new opportunities and develop their skills. These events often feature workshops, panel discussions, and networking opportunities with recruiters and industry professionals. Students can use these events to learn about different industries, develop their networking skills, and even secure internships or job offers.

  Finally, students can also benefit from seeking out mentors and career coaches who can provide them with personalized guidance and support as they navigate the job market. Mentors can offer valuable insights, advice, and feedback that can help students make informed decisions and set realistic goals for their career development. Career coaches, on the other hand, can provide students with tools and strategies for developing their skills, building their professional network, and achieving their career goals.

  There are a variety of resources available to students who are looking to further explore and develop their marketable skills. By taking advantage of online courses, professional organizations, career fairs, and mentors, students can continue to grow and develop their skills in a way that will make them stand out in the competitive job market. By investing time and effort into their professional development, students can position themselves for success and achieve their career goals.

www.ingramcontent.com/pod-product-compliance
Lightning Source LLC
Chambersburg PA
CBHW070208230526
45471CB00002B/867